LUKE

THEOLOGY OF WORK PROJECT

LUKE

THE BIBLE AND YOUR WORK
Study Series

 HENDRICKSON PUBLISHERS

Theology of Work
The Bible and Your Work Study Series: Luke

© 2014 by Hendrickson Publishers Marketing, LLC
P.O. Box 3473
Peabody, Massachusetts 01961-3473

ISBN 978-1-61970-515-9

William Messenger, Executive Editor, Theology of Work Project
Sean McDonough, Biblical Editor, Theology of Work Project
Patricia Anders, Editorial Director, Hendrickson Publishers

Contributors:
Jo Kadlecek, "Luke" Bible Study
Aaron Kuecker, "Luke and Work" in the *Theology of Work Bible Commentary*

The Theology of Work Project is an independent, international organization dedicated to researching, writing, and distributing materials with a biblical perspective on work. The Project's primary mission is to produce resources covering every book of the Bible plus major topics in today's workplaces. Wherever possible, the Project collaborates with other faith-and-work organizations, churches, universities, and seminaries to help equip people for meaningful, productive work of every kind.

Printed in the United States of America

First Printing – November 2014

Contents

The Theology of Work

Work is not only a human calling but also a divine one. "In the beginning God created the heavens and the earth." God worked to create us and created us to work. "The LORD God took the man and put him in the garden of Eden to till it and keep it" (Gen. 2:15). God also created work to be good, even if it's hard to see in a fallen world. To this day, God calls us to work to support ourselves and to serve others (Eph. 4:28).

Work can accomplish many of God's purposes for our lives—the basic necessities of food and shelter, as well as a sense of fulfillment and joy. Our work can create ways to help people thrive. Our work can discover the depths of God's creation. Our work can bring us into wonderful relationships with co-workers and those who benefit from our work (customers, clients, patients, and so forth).

Yet many people face drudgery, boredom, or exploitation at work. We have bad bosses, hostile relationships, and unfriendly work environments. Our work seems useless, unappreciated, faulty, frustrating. We don't get paid enough. We get stuck in dead-end jobs or laid off or fired. We fail. Our skills become obsolete. It's a struggle just to make ends meet. But how can this be if God created work to be good—and what can we do about it? God's answers to these questions must be somewhere in the Bible, but where?

The Theology of Work Project's mission has been to study what the Bible says about work and to develop resources to apply the Christian faith to our work. It turns out that every book of the Bible gives practical, relevant guidance that can help us do our jobs better, improve our relationships at work, support ourselves, serve others more effectively, and find meaning and value in our work. The Bible shows us how to live all of life—including work—in Christ. Only in Jesus can our work be transformed to become the blessing it was always meant to be.

To put it another way, if we are not following Christ during the 100,000 hours of our lives that we spend at work, are we really following Christ? Our lives are more than just one day a week at church. The fact is that God cares about our life *every day of the week*. But how do we become equipped to follow Jesus at work? In the same ways we become equipped for every aspect of life in Christ—listening to sermons, modeling our lives on others' examples, praying for God's guidance, and most of all by studying the Bible and putting it into practice.

This Theology of Work series contains a variety of books to help you apply the Scriptures and Christian faith to your work. This Bible study is one volume in the series The Bible and Your Work. It is intended for those who want to explore what the Bible says about work and how to apply it to their work in positive, practical ways. Although it can be used for individual study, Bible study is especially effective with a group of people committed to practicing what they read in Scripture. In this way, we gain from one another's perspectives and are encouraged to actually *do* what we read in Scripture. Because of the direct focus on work, The Bible and Your Work studies are especially suited for Bible studies *at* work or *with* other people in similar occupations. The following lessons are designed for thirty-minute lunch breaks (or perhaps breakfast before work) during a five-day work week.

Christians today recognize God's calling to us in and through our work—for ourselves and for those whom we serve. May God use this book to help you follow Christ in every sphere of life and work.

Will Messenger, Executive Editor
Theology of Work Project

Chapter 1

God's Kingdom at Work

Lesson #1: A Loving King (Luke 1–4)

Introduction to the Gospel of Luke

Anyone about to enter today's workforce usually begins with two questions: Who's in charge and what's the goal? Both define the culture of a workplace, creating a vision and mission from which every aspect of the organization operates.

In many ways that is exactly what is happening in the Gospel of Luke. Across each page, we hear Jesus proclaimed as the king, the one in charge of a world governed by those who don't recognize God's authority. From his mission, Christ then establishes a new culture—what Luke calls the "kingdom"—that reflects God's deep concern for every aspect of a person's life, from work, money, and governance to justice, compassion, and character. In fact, Luke—who was also a doctor—uses his gifts of observation to provide details of God's strategic plan, carefully describing not only who's in charge but what that means for Christ's followers.

As you begin to study this rich and historic account of Christ's time on earth, you'll notice how Jesus is both the king and model for all those who hold authority. While many contemporary readers might think of him primarily as the founder of a religion, Luke demonstrates that Jesus is much more than that. From Christ's birth in a stable—where wise men worshipped the newborn king—to his death and resurrection, Luke tells the story of the true king who has come to a broken world to reestablish God's original intentions. Even Satan and his minions acknowledge Jesus' rule (Luke 8:32) because his power cannot be challenged. But unlike the self-serving emperors and kings around him, Jesus uses his power to sacrifice himself for the good of others.

 Food for Thought

Reflect for a moment on this idea of power motivated by love. How does this fit with your view of authority? What other themes do you expect to find as you explore the Gospel of Luke?

_____

_____

_____

_____

_____

_____

_____

Jesus' Job Description (Luke 1:26–56; 4:14–22)

It might seem strange for God to announce his plan to establish his kingdom in the midst of two workplaces, but he did. First, he speaks through an angel in the temple where Zechariah was ministering (Luke 1:8), then in the fields where shepherds are herding their flocks (Luke 2:9).

It might seem even stranger that God introduces Jesus with a job description. But through the angel Gabriel, he tells Mary she is to give birth to a son who "will be great, and will be called the Son of the Most High, and the Lord God will give to him the throne of his ancestor David. He will reign over the house of Jacob forever, and of his kingdom there will be no end" (Luke 1:32–33).

From these starting points, we'll see later how Jesus fulfills his "job description" as king as he performs great miracles, challenges the proud, lifts up the humble, and confronts the corrupt rulers of the time. In stark contrast to the movers and shakers of his time, Jesus uses his power to benefit the most vulnerable. He doesn't need to schmooze with the powerful or wealthy. He does not oppress his people or tax them to support luxurious habits. He establishes a properly governed realm where everyone can prosper and live in peace. He cares for people in every station and condition, as we will see. But his concern for the poor, the suffering, and the powerless distinguishes him starkly from the rulers he has come to displace.

 Food for Thought

Read through the following passage that Jesus quotes from Isaiah 61:1–2 after he spent forty days in the wilderness:

> "The Spirit of the Lord is upon me,
>   because he has anointed me
>   to bring good news to the poor.
> He has sent me to proclaim release to the captives
>   and recovery of sight to the blind,
>   to let the oppressed go free,
>   to proclaim the year of the Lord's favor." (Luke 4:18–19)

What does this say about his leadership, and what you can expect to learn from Luke's Gospel? How might this passage inform your own sense of mission or purpose?

_____

_____

_____

_____

_____

_____

_____

_____

Prayer

Pause for a few moments of silence to reflect on what you've just studied. Then offer a prayer, either spontaneous or by using the following:

Lord,

Thank you for revealing your power in the person of Jesus, in Scripture, and in this place today through the Spirit of the Lord. May your love for me be my motivation to serve you and those around me so they might see your kingdom.

In Christ's name, amen.

Lesson #2: Called to the Kingdom (Luke 5:1–11)

New Recruits

Have you ever fantasized about quitting your job to pursue a "higher calling," such as ministry? "There is no higher calling than to be a pastor of the church," claims one seminary website. But Jesus doesn't say anything like that. When he calls people to follow, they do not change jobs to become ministers. The fishermen remain fishermen, and Jesus uses his power to help them do a better job of fishing (Luke 5:4–7). The tax collectors remain tax collectors (Luke 19:1–10), and Jesus helps them do a more ethical job of collecting taxes. Jesus himself is not called a minister (priest) but a king, prophet, and teacher (Luke 1:33, 76; 7:40). The higher calling from Jesus is not to get a job as a minister but to do your work—whatever it is—the way it should be done.

Let's look a bit deeper at Jesus' call to the fishermen in Luke 5:1–11. Jesus finishes speaking to the crowd and tells the fishermen, "'Put out into the deep water and let down your nets for a catch.' Simon answered, 'Master, we have worked all night long but have caught nothing. Yet if you say so, I will let down the nets.' When they had done this, they caught so many fish that their nets were beginning to break" (Luke 5:4–6). Simon is amazed that fishing is so important to Jesus, and he confesses that he has not been doing it with any thought to God's presence. "I am a sinful man!" he admits. But Jesus tells him that his fishing will be transformed into service to God nonetheless. "Do not be afraid; from now on you will be catching people" (Luke 5:11). Simon and his partners immediately abandon their boats so they can follow Jesus. But they do not cease being fishermen, and they put their boating skills to good use in Jesus' service (Luke 8:22–37).

 *Food for Thought*

What would it look like for Jesus to use his power to do amazing things in the work you do? What would have to change in your work for it to be a high calling? If you saw Jesus' power in your work, could that enable you to make those changes? What can you ask God for to elevate your work tomorrow?

_____

_____

_____

_____

_____

_____

_____

A Kingdom of Workers

Imagine you are on an airplane in the middle of take-off. What is the highest calling you can think of at that moment? Pilot? Jet mechanic? Imagine your toilet is overflowing and won't stop. Are you glad that all the plumbers haven't gone off to "higher callings"? Imagine you are in a spiritual crisis. Are you glad that God has set aside some people to be pastors? Imagine you are staying in a hotel, or trying to find a job, or lying in a hospital bed. What professions seem highest to you now?

As king, Jesus needs every kind of worker to make his kingdom productive, secure, and just. He needs people to cultivate God's creation, people to heal the world's hurts, people to redeem those who are lost. (The Bible itself gives an example of this in the many professions required in Solomon's kingdom; see 1 Kings 5–9.) We learn from Luke that Jesus called women, tax collectors, military officers, and others, and in some cases commanded them not to leave home and follow him (for example, Luke 8:29–39). God equips all of us for particular kinds of work in Christ's kingdom, and each job is equally important. Whatever our trade or profession, we can contribute our labor as God's kingdom is built.

 Food for Thought

British writer Dorothy L. Sayers once said that any secular vocation can be sacred work. "What the Church should be telling him [the carpenter] is this: that the very first demand that his religion makes upon him is that he should make good tables" ("Why Work?" in *Creed or Chaos?* [New York: Harcourt Brace, 1949]).

In other words, regardless of the work we do, each job can honor God if we do it well. How do you think that connects to what Jesus told the fisherman about fishing—that from now on they would become, as one Bible translation puts it, "fishers of men"?

Prayer

Pause to reflect in silence on what you have just studied. Then offer a prayer, either spontaneous or by using the following:

> *Lord,*
>
> *Thank you that you have called me to participate with you in building your kingdom right where I am. Help me to follow you and see you as infinitely more valuable than any success I may know.*
>
> *In Christ's name, amen.*

Lesson #3: Stories of Work in Jesus' Kingdom (Luke 13:6–21; 15:11–32)

One of Jesus' most famous ways of telling about his kingdom is the stories he told in parables. Each one reveals something about Jesus' kingdom, and the great majority of them are set in workplaces. In this lesson we will skip ahead a bit to explore four parables that reveal the creative and redemptive elements of work in Jesus' kingdom.

Stories of Productivity (Luke 13:6–21)

In the beginning, when the earth was a garden paradise, God gave people the responsibility to grow his creation's productive capacity and harvest its abundance (Gen. 1:28–30). God chose to use our work to fulfill his creative design for the world. Jesus' parables of the fig tree, the mustard seed, and yeast show that we still have this responsibility and that our productivity still matters to God.

The parable in Luke 13:6–9 tells of a man who plants a fig tree, which after three years still bears no fruit. "Cut it down!" he tells his gardener. "Why should it be wasting the soil?" Perhaps the fig tree represents the earth's resources or perhaps it represents us. Either way, the point is that God's purpose for his creation and his creatures is to grow and bring forth fruit. But God has patience. The gardener says, "Sir, let it alone for one more year, until I dig around it and put manure on it." Perhaps the gardener is Jesus, tending to us, or perhaps we are the gardeners, tending to God's creation, or perhaps both. In either case, we see that an essential job in Jesus' kingdom is to cultivate creation's potential, both natural and human. To dig and fertilize is to grow food, educate students, fabricate steel, research nature, manage organizations, collect taxes (legitimately), paint pictures, make a profit, sew clothing, and other myriad jobs people do to create and produce what the world needs.

 Food for Thought

In the context of your work, do you find the parable of the fig tree threatening or affirming? On the one hand, it depicts a bleak future for the unproductive, but on the other it shows a masterful gardener cultivating the tree's hidden potential. Of course, getting manure dumped on you isn't necessarily pleasant. What hardships do you face in the pursuit of productivity?

_____

_____

_____

_____

The parable of the mustard seed in Luke 13:18–19 is similar. "What is the kingdom of God like? And to what should I compare it? It is like a mustard seed that someone took and sowed in the garden; it grew and became a tree, and the birds of the air made nests in its branches." Someone's work turned a tiny seed into an abundant habitat. The parable of yeast in Luke 13:20–21 reiterates the point. "To what should I compare the kingdom of God? It is like yeast that a woman took and mixed in with three measures of flour until all of it was leavened." Skillful use of God's creation enables workers to feed a population that would otherwise go hungry and pass from the earth.

Of course, these parables are not about gardening and baking. They do not teach agricultural techniques or kitchen recipes. And they are not only about increasing the world's physical productivity. They are also metaphors for growing the kingdom of God by inviting people to follow Jesus. But they affirm that our daily work is founded on God's command to produce what is needed for human flourishing, to increase our science and skill, and to care for God's creation.

 Food for Thought

Does the smallness of the mustard seed relate to you and your work? How about the results, which are said to benefit the birds of the air, without mentioning benefits to the person who planted the seed?

_____

_____

_____

_____

How about the parable of the yeast? Leavening bread requires the scientific knowledge—or at least the practical training—to mix together optimal proportions, inoculate the dough with the proper microorganisms, control the pH, humidity, and temperature, and knead the dough at the right time. What knowledge and skills are required for your work? How does that benefit the people who use the products of your work?

_____

_____

_____

_____

_____

A Story of Generosity (Luke 15:11–32)

While the parable of the prodigal son offers a kaleidoscope of insights, we'll focus on just one facet—how to use money wisely. Using money generously to foster good relationships turns out to be the key.

The younger son begins with a shockingly ungenerous demand to his father—give me the money now that I'm going to inherit when you die. He selfishly uses his father's money to break off his relationship with his father. Squabbles over money have destroyed many families, but few have begun with such blatant hostility. The son goes to "a distant country" where he'll never have to see his father again and soon squanders all his money. The term "dissolute living" suggests that he tries to use his money to compensate for his lack of genuine relationships. But as soon as the money is gone, there is no one to help him in the hard times that follow. Then he remembers there is one relationship that might yet survive—the one with his father. There may be just enough fondness left there to keep him from starving.

In contrast, the father is wise in generosity. He throws everything he has into the service of rebuilding his relationship with his son— the finest clothing, the best food, a ring for his hand. He uses it all to say, "I love you." The son is amazed by his father's generosity, and it does indeed restore the love that had been lost. "This son of mine was dead and is alive again," the father says. "He was lost and is found!" Love, expressed through generosity, leads to a complete transformation. "And they began to celebrate."

In the presence of his father's life-giving generosity, however, the older brother wants only to complain. He refuses to take part in the celebration. It's understandable that he's angry at his brother, but his inability to rejoice in his father's generosity shuts him out of the happy ending that everyone else in the parable experiences. By refusing to accept the father's generosity to others, he makes himself miserable and lonely.

Generosity is a rich vein running through the Gospel of Luke, which we'll see come to the surface again in future chapters.

 Food for Thought

Three attitudes toward generosity are visible in the parable of the prodigal son. The younger son seems to be foolishly generous, spending his money on lavish parties and entertainment. The father is wisely generous, spending his money in support of his acts of love and relationship-building. The older son is not generous at all, it seems, and even opposes the generosity of his father. Which of these attitudes toward generosity is closest to yours? What role would you like generosity to have in your life, your relationships, and your work? How much would it cost? Where do your attitudes and habits about the use of money come from?

_____

_____

_____

_____

How do you respond to generosity that you witness but are not directly involved in—the good fortune that comes to other people? Can you take delight in the unexpected promotion, the fortunate turn of events, and even the undeserved success that a colleague experiences? Or do you resent their success, as if someone else's good fortune must come at your expense? Learning to take delight in the bounty that falls to other people seems to be important to Jesus in these parables in Luke. Why is that?

_____

_____

_____

_____

_____

Prayer

Pause to reflect in silence on what you have just studied. Then offer a prayer, either spontaneous or by using the following:

Lord,

Make me productive and creative in your kingdom. Give me a spirit of generosity and the wisdom to put everything I have to use in the service of loving other people.

Amen.

Chapter 2

God's Kingdom and Workplace Ethics

Lesson #1: Why Ethics Matters at Work (Luke 3:8–14)

Personal Ethics

When Susan was passed over for promotion, she felt sure it was because she didn't socialize with her boss after work the way the person who got the promotion did. This felt unfair to Susan, but she soon learned that no one else in the company was interested in helping her fight the decision. Supposedly the other candidate had higher performance reviews, although Susan didn't see any evidence of that herself. It felt even more unfair that Susan was asked to do more out of town travel now that her former rival had been promoted. Her husband wasn't happy about the extra travel either.

One day, surfing the Internet in her hotel room, Susan found tickets for a playoff game back home the day she was returning. She bought the tickets and surprised her husband by taking him to the game that night. He loved it, and it really helped soften his unhappiness about Susan's extra travel. From then on, every time she traveled on business, she bought her husband an expensive surprise, and he began looking forward to her trips. She found that it was much easier than she expected to disguise the gifts on her expense account, so that her company ended up paying for them. She knew it was against the rules—a kind of stealing, actually—but it felt justifiable to her. The company had cheated her out of a promotion she deserved, and the gifts were only making up for the extra travel she was being forced to do. If the company paid a bit extra for her to keep the peace with her husband, what did it really matter?

But it does matter. As we consider developing a set of kingdom ethics for the workplace, we have to see that every compromised decision—no matter how small it might seem—has consequences, usually in financial terms. In fact, the first teaching in Luke comes from John the Baptist, rather than Jesus, and deals specifically with ethical issues on the job. When the crowds ask John how to "bear fruits worthy of repentance" (Luke 3:8), he tells the soldiers, "Be satisfied with your wages" (Luke 3:14), and the tax collectors, "Collect no more than the amount prescribed for you" (Luke 3:13). Workers are not to use their power or cunning to cheat others but to be content with their legitimate pay.

In other words, understanding God's call on our lives includes ethical practices in the workplace that affect our view of money and power. Susan might have viewed padding her expense account as a little way of getting back at her company for not promoting her as she thought she deserved. Few people are consciously unethical, but all of us are tempted to get away with small shortcuts we think will give us what we are owed. But is that really any different from a tax agent demanding a bribe or a soldier looting a store? Ethical lapses start small, but they grow larger the longer we get away with them.

 *Food for Thought*

In Luke 3:8, John the Baptist tells his audience to bear fruit worthy of repentance and then gives examples of ethics at work. Are there things you do at work that you'd prefer others not know about? What kinds of small lapses do you see around you? Are you ever tempted? What could you do to help yourself resist the temptation to little ethical lapses?

_____

_____

_____

_____

Social Ethics

John the Baptist goes beyond telling people not to cheat, steal, or lie at work. Not only are we to avoid unethical behavior, but we are also to use our work and our wealth to serve others. Those whose hearts are humbled by God's grace are to serve others first, irrespective of their profession or status. John tells those with plenty of clothing and food to share with those who have nothing (Luke 3:10). If you have the ability (for example, extra clothes or food) to help others in need, you are called to do so.

Social duty also emerges from a deeper look at John's commands to the soldiers and tax collectors. The job of soldiers is to protect the populace, but soldiers who extract bribes from the citizenry soon neglect their military duties in order to focus on extortion. For example, in AD 408, the Roman army besieged the city of Rome, demanding a large ransom in exchange for returning to their proper duties. Meanwhile, the empire's enemies continued their advance, and two years later the Visigoths sacked the city.

Likewise with the tax collectors. Trumped-up taxes throughout Palestine not only enriched unethical tax collectors, but they also gave a pretext for corrupt officials to confiscate the land of anyone who couldn't pay the inflated amount. The patchwork of small family-owned farms and pastures that had existed for generations was replaced by large estates owned by politically connected elites and operated by slaves. Tax collectors not only padded their own purses, but they also played into the wholesale destruction of Palestine's economic system. This was the way of the world during the Roman occupation of Israel and Judea, but workers who obeyed God were called to be different.

John the Baptist's social ethics, then, embrace both generosity with our money and possessions and working for the good of society, rather than merely enriching ourselves. Those who want to serve God are to view justice as both their standard and their guide as to conducting their professional affairs. The good of others lies at the center of their ethics.

 Food for Thought

When John says that those who own two coats must share with anyone who has none, is he speaking to you? If he is, how could you specifically fulfill his command? When John talks to soldiers and tax collectors about doing their jobs for the benefit of society, is he talking to you? How does doing your job ethically benefit society? What small ethical lapses occur in your occupation that actually contribute to major social problems?

_____

_____

_____

_____

Prayer

Pause to reflect in silence on John's mission. Then offer a prayer, either spontaneous or by using the following:

> *Righteous God,*
>
> *Only you can make me righteous through Christ, and only you can help me remain as focused as John was on doing what you've called me to do at work—bear fruit worthy of repentance. Thank you that you are with me, even when it is difficult to do the right thing.*
>
> *Amen.*

Lesson #2: Working Beside Temptation (Luke 4:1–13)

Who's Really in Charge?

Just before he began his work as king, Jesus was tempted to abandon his allegiance to God. While he was preparing and fasting for forty days in the wilderness, Satan taunted Jesus with a series of temptations that also questioned Christ's very authority: "If you are the Son of God, command this stone to become a loaf of bread" (Luke 4:3); "If you, then, will worship me, it [power and glory] will all be yours" (Luke 4:5–8); and "If you are the Son of God, throw yourself down from here [the temple]" (Luke 4:9–12). Each time, Christ responded with the truth of Scripture, reminding Satan that God is in charge.

Every kind of work has temptations. Our power to resist them does not rest in our inherent goodness or our strength of character, but from recognizing that God is in charge. The question is not whether we are good enough or strong enough to resist temptation, but whether giving in to temptation will help us or harm us. If we are masters of our own lives and work, then giving in to temptation is good for us. We could use our power to gain security, power, fame, and self-sufficiency. In that case, resisting temptation means choosing not to do things that will benefit us greatly. Can we really expect to resist that kind of temptation for a lifetime?

But if God is in charge, then giving in to temptations is actually bad for us. Making more money and getting more stuff does not actually make us more secure, because "one does not live by bread alone" (Luke 4:4). If we get the bread but lose our relationships with God and other people, giving in to the temptation of money will actually make us less secure, not more. Likewise, gaining power by partnering with unethical people and organizations actually makes us more vulnerable, not less. Not only are the good guys trying to stop us, but our own partners are also ever ready to stab us in the back. And if we give in to the temptation of self-sufficiency—of not recognizing that God is with us in our work—we actually become less capable of doing effective work. Our gifts and skills come from God, and when we cut ourselves off from him, they begin to wither and amount to nothing.

Recognizing that God is in charge of our work begins with our attitude toward God—"Worship the Lord your God"—which has immediate, practical effects in our work—"and serve only him" (Luke 4:8). If our attitude is that God is in charge, then the work we do to serve him will benefit ourselves and others. If our attitude is that we are in charge, then the work we do to serve ourselves will bring us to ruin and will harm those around us.

 *Food for Thought*

What temptations do you face in your work? How do you resist them, and how successful have you been? In situations where you have given in to temptation, what have been the results for yourself and others? Is it true that doing your work as service to God makes you less susceptible to temptation?

_____

_____

_____

_____

_____

_____

The Protection of Preparation

It's not hard to see how Satan's three questions relate to today's workplace. First, we often think we must work to meet only our own needs or that our work alone is our provider. But work is more than either—we're meant to serve others through our work, no matter how tempted we might be to take shortcuts or to ignore the burden our poor work habits might place on others.

In the same way, we might question God's presence and power when we're on the job, just as Jesus was tempted to test God by forcing his hand. Sometimes, if we're lazy or foolish, we expect God will pull off some great superhero rescue for us. Or worse, we come to believe that God is not interested in our work, that all that matters to him is church life. What right do we have to ask him for help when we're in the office?

But as Jesus prepared for his calling as king, God's Spirit led him into the desert where he gave him power, wisdom, and assurance before he began. Satan's temptations came to him—as they do to us—without warning. Yet because Jesus had spent forty days in God's Spirit, he was fully prepared to resist. That's the secret to our success as well. We don't know when we'll be asked to submit a false report, when an unlocked door might tempt us to take something that isn't ours, or even when we might be tempted to join in a gossip session about a co-worker during our lunch break. But we do know that when we prepare—through prayer, fellowship, and studying God's word—we'll be protected from any temptation to act outside of God's standards. Put another way, as we nurture our communion with our heavenly Father, as Jesus did, in the power of his Holy Spirit, we too will be prepared and protected from any taunts that might come our way. His character will be formed in us.

 Food for Thought

All of us have our own temptations, large and small, depending on who we are, our circumstances, and the nature of our work. Obviously, we are not the Son of God, yet how we respond to temptation has life-changing consequences. What specific steps do you need to take in preparing the key to victory over any temptations that might come to you at work?

_____

_____

_____

_____

Prayer

Pause to reflect in silence on Christ's time in the wilderness. Then offer a prayer, either spontaneous or by using the following:

Lord Jesus,

Thank you that you overcame the temptation for power, luxury, and disbelief in God, so that we too could know your victory and presence in our lives and careers. May we be protected by the grace of your sacrifice and new life in us.

Amen.

Lesson #3: Serving Others in the Midst of Conflict (Luke 6:27–42; 17:3–4)

Surviving the Heat

All workplaces experience conflict. In Luke 6:27–28, Jesus addresses such situations of conflict with some counterintuitive wisdom: "Love your enemies, do good to those who hate you, bless those who curse you, pray for those who abuse you." With the colleague who seems intent on making us look bad, or the customer who's determined to vent anger on us, Jesus tells us to love. And not only to love but also to do good and bless those people who curse us, even pray for them! In other words, Jesus' advice for surviving the heat of conflict is to love and serve those we're in conflict with. As hard as it is to love those who oppose us, love is the heart of Jesus' way of resolving conflict.

Love, in conflict situations, does not mean stifling ourselves and playing nice on the outside while boiling over on the inside. Love requires being honest with ourselves and with others about the facts and feelings we perceive in the conflict. "If another disciple sins, you must rebuke the offender" (Luke 17:3). Speak up about what bothers you, but do it directly to the person in question, not to anyone else. The goal is not to apportion blame but to resolve the conflict, end any abuse, and restore a working relationship. If you can state your perspective respectfully, the other person may be able to see how this action harmed you and feel sorry about it. An apology is likely to follow. It can be surprisingly difficult, however, to accept someone else's apology, because doing so requires us to let go of an emotional stick to use against them in the future. But accepting a genuine apology is essential, for Jesus says, "If the same person sins against you seven times a day, and turns back to you seven times and says, 'I repent,' you must forgive" (Luke 17:4).

Forgiveness doesn't necessarily mean, though, that there are no consequences. If the other person lied or misled you, you can forgive yet still require the offender to set the record straight publicly or submit to greater scrutiny in the future. Or if you were abused, this should be reported to the authorities. Assuming the offender truly has repented, that person will welcome—or at least accept—corrective action. The forgiveness consists in letting go of malice and replacing it with practical love—a desire to do whatever is best for the other person going forward. Jesus' point is not leniency but good will. "Do to others as you would have them do to you" (Luke 6:31).

 Food for Thought

When conflict arises, Christians are not to crush others but rather build them up. Christ calls us to work for the good of those with whom we are in conflict, not to avoid conflict or withdraw from competition. How can you help those around you be their best, even if they might be competing with you? How can you forgive others—and be forgiven yourself—while still maintaining a culture of accountability?

_____

_____

_____

_____

_____

_____

The Log in Your Own Eye

We assumed above that the conflict was due to someone else's actions. When people do something that harms you, you bring it to their attention, they repent, and you forgive. But what if the conflict is due to your actions? We seldom recognize our role in creating conflicts, or, as Jesus asks, "Why do you see the speck of sawdust in your neighbor's eye, but do not notice the log in your own eye?" (Luke 6:41). In fact, most conflicts arise at least in part because of what we have done, not only because of what someone else did to us.

When facing conflict, therefore, don't assume that you are right and the other person wrong. "Do not judge," Jesus says (Luke 6:37). Listen to your brother's rebukes, open to the possibility that you, too, also have something to repent of. Once you have truly listened to each other, then one or both of you may realize you have something to apologize for. Both of you may owe each other an apology. Both of you may need to forgive yet hold the other person accountable. Both of you will need to develop a genuine care for each other going forward.

This brings us back to humility and grace. Humility comes from honest self-awareness so that whenever we feel heat or conflict, we first ask for God's grace in showing us our role in the situation. We're to seek out ways we can help those around us succeed, another practical way to "do to others as you would have them do to you" (Luke 6:31). It can be difficult to serve someone with whom you've been in conflict, but doing so reflects the Lord's own attitude of sacrifice and service as he establishes his kingdom for our sakes.

 Food for Thought

The touchstone of any ethical standard for Christians in the workplace is the hard work of forgiveness. Only God can help us let go of the wrongs we've done or experienced. When we do, we are free to restore good relationships and resolve conflicts. What conflicts have you experienced at work that were surprisingly hard to let go of? Are there people you would still rather despise than forgive? Is there any grace you need from God right now to resolve long-simmering conflicts?

_____

_____

_____

_____

_____

_____

Prayer

Pause to reflect in silence on Christ's grace and forgiveness. Then offer a prayer, either spontaneous or by using the following:

> Lord,
>
> *I pray that the Prince of Peace would reign in any conflict around me. Help me to reflect to others the same grace, love, and forgiveness you have offered me so that they may see you more clearly.*
>
> *Amen.*

Chapter 3

God's Kingdom and Working Attitudes

Lesson #1: The Hope of Health (Luke 4:31–44)

The Question of Suffering

Our last chapter described the ethics—or decision-making guidelines—for living in God's kingdom while we're at work. We're to
pursue what is good and just, prepare in advance to fight temptation, and be anchored in grace, humility, and forgiveness when
conflict arises. Now let's consider how our working attitudes,
formed from God's kingdom ethics, could reflect the same hope
that motivated Christ the king in all he did.

In Jesus' day (as in ours), the work of healing and health was
essential. Because Luke was also a physician, it's not surprising
that he recorded thirteen stories of Jesus healing people. In each
instance, Jesus reinforced his job description—that is, what he
had declared when he emerged from the wilderness and quoted
from Isaiah 61:1–2.

> "The Spirit of the Lord is upon me,
>   because he has anointed me
>   to bring good news to the poor.
> He has sent me to proclaim release to the captives
>   and recovery of sight to the blind,
>   to let the oppressed go free,
> to proclaim the year of the Lord's favor." (Luke 4:18–19)

Unlike the rulers of the fallen world, Jesus would rule on behalf of the sick, the poor, the blind, and the oppressed. Each time he healed someone, he confirmed his promise. In other words, his very attitude was one of deep concern for those in need. Everywhere he went, he ran into suffering people and brought wellness. To the man possessed by an unclean spirit, he gave freedom (Luke 4:31–37), and to Simon's mother-in-law suffering an illness and fever, he gave relief (Luke 4:38–44). With each healing, Jesus pointed to another kingdom, one where there would be no more sickness. And in the process, he modeled that God not only commands his followers to work for the benefit of others, but he also empowers them to do so because of what is to come.

 Food for Thought

Theologian Jürgen Moltmann beautifully sums up the reality that all healings depend on God's power: "Jesus' healings are not supernatural miracles in a natural world. They are the only truly 'natural' thing in a world that is unnatural, demonized, and wounded" (*The Way of Jesus Christ* [Minneapolis: Fortress Press, 1995]). They are a tangible sign that God is putting the world back to rights. How does the hope of this vision for restored health motivate you to care for others around you today?

_____

_____

_____

_____

_____

_____

Participating with the Great Physician

While the healings reported in the Gospels are generally miraculous, Christians' nonmiraculous efforts to restore human bodies can also be seen as extensions of Jesus' life-giving ministry. And with technological advances, Christ's passion to alleviate suffering takes on new life.

For years, Sarah was plagued with arthritis in her hip. But as a high school history teacher and an active member of her local church, she struggled to keep up the pace that public education and community life demanded of her. No matter what she tried, the arthritis only got worse and managing the pain depleted her, taking away energy she needed for her students. Her work was compromised because of her health—until she met a leading orthopedic specialist who was able to diagnose and schedule a hip replacement surgery. Within months, she was back on the job, marveling that she lived in a time when the creative works of modern medicine could restore her quality of life—and work—so quickly. For Sarah, her faith in God's provision was deepened because of the doctors who cared for her.

It would be a mistake, then, not to notice how important healing is to the redemptive work of God's kingdom. This work is performed daily by health professionals such as Sarah encountered—doctors, nurses, technicians, claims processors, hospital parking lot attendants, and countless others whose work makes healing possible. But it would also be a mistake to infer that the healing professions are inherently higher callings than other professions. The point is that the kingdom of God is about physical, emotional, and spiritual wellness—both now and in the life to come.

 *Food for Thought*

If God's concern is for those who suffer, Christ's followers also share this concern and become his hands in caring for others. Compassion literally means "to suffer with" or to come alongside those who are hurting. In what ways can you offer compassion to those with whom you work or help colleagues respond to those in need beyond your workplace?

_____

_____

_____

_____

_____

_____

_____

_____

Prayer

Pause to reflect in silence on Christ's commitment to eliminate suffering. Then offer a prayer, either spontaneous or by using the following:

Lord,

Thank you for becoming a suffering servant on the cross for my sake, and for the sake of the world. Please help me to be your hands in caring for others with compassion and hope of the life to come.

Amen.

Lesson #2: The Power of Persistence (Luke 18:1–8)

Keeping At It

Christ's attitude reflected a deep concern for those who suffered. Everywhere he went during his time on earth, he encountered people who were sick, diseased, and often marginalized as a result. Yet Jesus knew it was not supposed to be like this, and so he never wavered in his commitment to bringing God's kingdom to the hurting.

In the parable that Christ tells in Luke 18:1–8, we meet a widow who, like Jesus, is determined not to give up. She is poor and powerless, yet she persistently prods a corrupt and powerful judge to do justice for her. Of course, the parable assumes that holding a position of leadership and power means you're also obligated to work on behalf of the weak and the poor. But that's not Christ's point in the story. Instead, he takes the parable in a different direction by calling us "to pray always and not to lose heart" (Luke 18:1).

Caring for others can be tiring work, and Jesus pursuing justice or working for any other kingdom endeavor would require God's strength and persistence. Staying focused in the midst of challenges or disappointments is not easy, and yet the sheer act of stick-to-itiveness is crucial for accomplishing the tasks we've been given to do.

 *Food for Thought*

We can assume Jesus was using the parable to show that if persistence can pay off with a corrupt human of limited power, imagine how much more with a just God of infinite power! What does the lesson of persistence and prayer mean for you right now?

_____

_____

_____

_____

_____

_____

Staying the Course

Today's work culture doesn't always make it easy to work according to Christian values, much less to acknowledge faith in God as their source. But the parable of the persistent widow encourages today's Christ-followers to press on in their faith, even when the odds are stacked against them. It challenges us to remember that even within the corrupt or demoralizing systems of our world, God's will is at work no matter what. That is our hope and what helps us stay the course. And that hope is what others see in our attitudes on the job.

Yet notice how God did not directly intervene in the parable of the persistent widow. The widow's persistence alone led the judge to relent and finally to act justly. Here Jesus seems to imply that God is the unseen actor. "Will not God grant justice to his chosen ones who cry to him day and night?" (Luke 18:8).

Regardless of our vocation, Christians can be confident that God will indeed bring about justice in a corrupt world. In the same way that God can bring miraculous healing into a sick world, we can be sure that he is able to bring miraculous justice to corrupt industries or wrongful deeds. That is why we are instructed to pray and not to lose heart, to come consistently to God so as not to give up in our work. And though we cannot right every wrong in our lifetimes, we can persistently create opportunities that point to the hope of God's kingdom.

 Food for Thought

This short but powerful parable encourages us to never stop working for the greater good. No matter what happens, our hope in Christ's work on the cross keeps us moving ahead. How does Christ's hope inspire you to keep going in your faith, regardless of your profession?

_____

_____

_____

_____

_____

_____

_____

Prayer

Pause to reflect in silence on the widow's persistence in deed and in word. Then offer a prayer, either spontaneous or by using the following:

> *God of Hope,*
>
> *When I feel like giving up, please change my attitude and strengthen my faith in you so that others might be encouraged to know you.*
>
> *Amen.*

Lesson #3: The Responsibility of Risk (Luke 19:11–27)

Return on Investment

It's a dramatic, high-stakes environment—the world of financial services. The point, of course, is to invest in such a way as to yield a profit for the client, and ultimately the broker. That's part of what's happening in the parable of the ten minas, or pounds of silver, which Jesus tells just before heading into Jerusalem. A rich nobleman is about to go on a trip where he will gain even more power as he is "promoted" as king. The problem is that few of those under him like him, knowing he is a harsh man and likely to be an even harsher ruler. Nonetheless, he puts ten servants (or slaves) in charge of a pound each and assigns them to invest his money while he's away. (The money would be several months' wages for an average laborer.) Two take a risk and invest the master's money so that it gains a handsome return for him. But the third servant is not so bold; his attitude of fear means that the only place to deposit his pound is in a safe place.

When the new king comes back, he gives a performance review to all three servants. The two who turned a profit from their risky investments are promoted and given a bonus check. But the third servant, the one who played it safe, is berated for being unproductive with the king's resources. The pound he failed to invest is then given to the servant who had earned the greatest return on his money. "I tell you, to all those who have, more will be given; but from those who have nothing, even what they have will be taken away" (Luke 19:26). The story concludes with harsh punishment for those who actually obstructed—rather than merely failing to invest in—the king's plans.

The parable is set in terms of financial transactions, and it certainly highlights the value of investing in growth, rather than simply stowing away wealth unproductively. Yet the story is not really about financial investment, but about using the resources at our disposal for God's purposes. If we use the wealth we have to invest in companies, organizations, ideas, and things that provide something of value in the world, we are serving Christ as king. The same is true of nonfinancial resources, including our gifts and skills, our time, our creativity, and our love.

 Food for Thought

This parable makes explicit that citizens of God's kingdom are responsible to work toward God's goals and purposes. In what way is your work an investment in God's kingdom? Which goals and purposes of God are furthered by your work?

_____

_____

_____

_____

Risky Business

Jesus tells this parable immediately before going to Jerusalem, where he is to be hailed as king but soon is rejected by his people. This identifies Jesus with the nobleman in the parable, and the crowd shouting "Crucify him!" (Luke 23:21) with the people in the parable who oppose the nobleman's coronation. In this context, the parable warns us that we must decide whether Jesus is indeed God's appointed king. That means there are considerable consequences we must weigh when choosing whether to serve him or oppose him. In other words, the parable makes it clear that citizens of God's kingdom are responsible for working toward God's goals and purposes, even if that requires an element of risk on our parts, regardless of what field we're in.

Just as the nobleman in the story makes it clear what he expects of his servants, so too does the Lord with those who follow and trust him. If we accept Jesus as king, we must expect to lead risky lives. Certainly, those in the story who invested the master's money faced the possibility of being attacked by those around them who rejected the new king's authority. They faced the risk of disappointing their master by losing money on their investments. And even their success exposed them to risk. Would they become greedy or power-hungry now that they'd received such promotions? Or would they respond with attitudes of humility and gratitude?

In short, neither failure nor success is safe in this parable, just as neither is in what we're called to do in today's workplace. Our jobs are not to duck for cover and look for the easy way of accommodating the system while waiting for things to improve. In fact, that's the one action in the story that Jesus condemns! The servant who tries to avoid risk is singled out as unfaithful. Rather, the parable implies that all investments made in faithful service to God please him, whether or not they achieve their intended payoff.

Food for Thought

Many of today's workplaces are a lot like this parable. You can get punished for mediocre results, which gives you an incentive to take greater risks in the hope of accomplishing more—a higher sales forecast, say, or a more innovative product. But if your risky idea fails, you can get blamed for making a big mistake. Who, then, do you most identify with in this parable? What risks might God be calling you to take for his purposes and for his kingdom?

_____

_____

_____

_____

_____

_____

_____

Prayer

Pause to reflect in silence on the role trust plays in taking risks for Christ. Then offer a prayer, either spontaneous or by using the following:

King Jesus,

Thank you for being so trustworthy that you would risk all on the cross for my sake. Help me to invest the gifts and resources you have given me in ways that cause your kingdom to flourish.

Amen.

Chapter 4

God's Kingdom and Sabbath Rest

Lesson #1: The Rhythm of Work and Rest (Luke 6:1–11)

Downtime

Joanne loved working with people, especially people in trouble, and she was eager to apply for a position in the credit-counseling department of a mortgage bank. With her finance background, she believed she could help people who were behind on their mortgage payments to keep their homes. In the interview, she learned that she would have to work every other weekend, including Sunday mornings. She had always kept from working on Sunday and attended church faithfully. Yet she also felt this job was a great way to use her gifts serving others.

Joanne's dilemma is how to observe a biblical command known as Sabbath rest. In Luke's Gospel, Jesus teaches and lives out the reality that work and rest are not opposing forces. He shows how a foundational understanding of the Sabbath makes both good work and true recreation possible.

Consider, for instance, the passage we come to now. On the Sabbath day, Jesus and his disciples are wandering through a field and they're hungry. So they pluck heads of grain, rub them in their hands, and eat the kernels. True to form, some Pharisees complain that they're not keeping the sacred rule to refrain entirely from work on the Sabbath. Jesus counters by reminding them that David and his companions ate consecrated bread in God's house—something lawful only for the priests—to meet their basic human needs. Human need does not conveniently disappear in the face of religious regulations. Decisions about how to observe the Sabbath must take into account both human needs and God's setting aside of a day for rest.

 Food for Thought

In his reasoning about meeting human needs on the Sabbath, Christ points to Scripture when David apparently broke another religious commandment. Yet God himself observed the Sabbath (Gen. 2:2–3) and commanded people to do the same (Exod. 20:8–11). What does Sabbath rest mean to you?

_____

_____

_____

_____

_____

Commandment of the Heart

The Pharisees did not hesitate to issue a religious judgment against Jesus and his disciples. Obviously, they didn't realize who they were talking to. Jesus answered with a familiar example, the story of his ancestor David, and at first glance it seems he was making a connection between two stories on hunger—almost implying that when we're hungry we should indeed work to feed ourselves, even if it's working on the Sabbath. But Jesus is saying something much more astounding. Jesus is claiming to be the

definitive authority on what Sabbath observance means. And in
his eyes, it begins from the premise that the Sabbath is there to
bless people, not the other way round.

Not only is he challenging their tightly held religious traditions
by boldly claiming to be Lord of the Sabbath, but he is also suggesting that keeping the Sabbath is more a matter of understanding God's heart than it is obeying detailed rules. David, after all,
was known as a "man after God's heart." And though keeping
the Sabbath is one of the Ten Commandments, Christ here helps
us understand that its importance has as much to do with our
hearts as it does with setting aside a day for rest. Both are to
honor God.

 Food for Thought

Imagine how Jesus' followers and the Pharisees might have responded when they heard Christ's claim, "The Son of Man is lord
of the sabbath" (Luke 6:5). How do you respond to his statement,
and how can you obey God's command for Sabbath with both
your heart and your schedule?

_____

_____

_____

_____

_____

_____

_____

Prayer

Pause to reflect in silence on the benefit of setting aside time for Sabbath rest. Then offer a prayer, either spontaneous or by using the following:

> *Lord of the Sabbath,*
>
> *Thank you for inviting me to rest in you so that you may work in me that which pleases you.*
>
> In the name of the Son of Man, amen.

Lesson #2: The Problem of Sabbath (Luke 13:10–17)

Breathing Room

We know from our last lesson that Christ claimed that "the Son of Man is lord of the sabbath" (Luke 6:5). With such a recognized sacred day in the Jewish religion, Jesus was both honoring the Sabbath and bringing a new perspective to it. Yes, he was reminding listeners that it was a commandment that required obedience, but he also implied that there was also freedom in keeping it.

Now we come to another story about Jesus and the Sabbath— only this one is set in a synagogue, the very place of worship for the people of Israel. He is a guest rabbi so he is not in charge of the order of service. And when he spots a crippled woman—someone vulnerable both as a female and a disabled person—Jesus again shows what the Sabbath is for: meeting the needs of people.

He calls her forward in front of the congregation, declares her
whole, and then touches her so she can stand up to praise God.
By doing so, he restores her to God's original intention for her—
good health. He frees her. But by doing so, he also invites tension
from the indignant synagogue leader who chastises the woman
and the crowd with religious language: "There are six days on
which work ought to be done; come on those days and be cured,
and not on the sabbath day" (Luke 13:14).

 Food for Thought

Consider the different responses between the synagogue ruler
and Jesus toward the crippled woman. What do they reveal to
you about Christ's priorities?

_____

_____

_____

_____

_____

_____

Free for All

Obviously, Jesus has different ideas than the religious leaders
on the purpose of the Sabbath. True, this story of healing on the
Sabbath—and others that Luke describes—doesn't necessarily
form a theology that keeping Sabbath is for healing. But it does
reflect what matters most to Jesus about the idea behind keeping Sabbath—that meeting the real needs of people fulfills the
Sabbath.

Consider his response to the leader's challenge, first by mentioning the laws with which these people would have surely been familiar, and then by adding another dimension to what they'd just witnessed. "Ought not this woman, a daughter of Abraham whom Satan bound for eighteen long years, be set free from this bondage on the sabbath day?" (Luke 13:16). Not only does he publically affirm this woman, but he also reinforces the primary purpose of the Lord of the Sabbath—freedom!

By setting aside time to come to the place of worship with others, the woman encountered the living God and gained the freedom and restoration she had sought for eighteen years. We can find freedom and restoration in Christ too. Christ's freedom for her, and for us, is at the heart of fulfilling the Sabbath.

 Food for Thought

Imagine what this woman felt as she shuffled toward Jesus in the synagogue and then when he freed her from her bondage. Which part of her story most resonates with you at this time in your life? What has Sabbath worship meant to you lately?

_____

_____

_____

_____

_____

_____

_____

_____

Prayer

Pause to reflect in silence on the benefit of gathering with others for Sabbath worship and rest. Then offer a prayer, either spontaneous or by using the following:

> *Lord of the Sabbath,*
>
> *Thank you for calling me to yourself and for fulfilling the Sabbath. Help me to praise you in freedom and to rest in you every day.*
>
> *Amen.*

Lesson #3: The Face of Sabbath (Luke 10:38–42)

Generous Service

By now we know that Christ considered the Sabbath an opportunity to care for the needs of others, while inviting them into relationship with him. He fed the hungry (physically and spiritually) and gave freedom to those who had been in bondage. It was a whole new way of thinking about rest and work, and it reflected a level of compassion many had never experienced before.

Though this story of the two sisters in Luke 10 does not directly mention the Sabbath, it does provide the face of God's priorities toward his people. Martha and Mary were friends with Christ, so when he visited them at their home, they naturally offered him hospitality. The problem was that Martha thought that serving him should look one way and Mary thought of it in another way. Martha became busy and distracted, while Mary sat quietly at his feet.

Unfortunately, many people throughout church history have made Martha out to be a poster child for all that is wrong with busyness. Some even consider her constant motion inferior to those who would see contemplation or monastic lifestyles— which Mary models—as more important. But this story must be read against the backdrop of the rest of Luke's Gospel, where the work of hospitality (a crucial form of generosity in the ancient Near East) is one of the key signs of God's kingdom breaking into the here and now, on the Sabbath and every other day.

 Food for Thought

The story of Martha and Mary puts generosity in the context of love for God. But the care they extend to Jesus is different. Which sister do you most identify with and why?

_____

_____

_____

_____

_____

_____

_____

The Necessity of Stillness

While Martha works to prepare dinner, Mary sits and listens to Jesus. Martha worries that her sister isn't doing enough to help her and then makes a bold request. She asks Jesus to rebuke Mary.

"Lord, do you not care that my sister has left me to do all the work by myself? Tell her then to help me" (Luke 10:40). But Jesus doesn't give her the answer she's expecting. Instead he commends Mary not for being busy like Martha but for sitting still!

Jesus doesn't minimize Martha's generous service, but he does remind her that her service needs to be grounded first in Mary's kind of love for him. Together, the sisters embody the type of generous lifestyles to which Jesus calls all of his followers. By sitting at his feet, Mary reflects how all our service and work must first be anchored in a lively personal relationship with him—that place where he feeds us and frees us to live as we were designed to live.

That place is a place of Sabbath, of sitting and listening, of resting from our busyness so that we emerge to give more to others as he gives to us. Following Christ—especially in today's fast-paced world—means becoming like Mary and Martha, where we learn to be quiet, generous, and loving, where we receive hospitality from the Son of Man so that we might offer it to others. Each of these elements of our life with him reinforces the other.

 Food for Thought

The story of Mary and Martha is not a story of incompatible lifestyles, but one that helps us better understand how to live in the tension of Sabbath. We're to rest at Christ's feet so that we might serve as he did. What practical steps could you take to worry less and listen more to the Lord of the Sabbath?

_____

_____

_____

_____

_____

_____

_____

_____

Prayer

Pause to reflect in silence on what it means to sit still with Christ. Then offer a prayer, either spontaneous or by using the following:

God of the Universe,

You are active and living and able to handle the cares of my heart and of those around me. Help me to sit with you so that I might reflect to others your compassion.

Amen.

Chapter 5

God's Kingdom and the Promise of Provision

Lesson #1: A Lot of Fish (Luke 9:10–17)

Seeing beyond the Obvious

Throughout Luke's Gospel, Jesus teaches that living in God's kingdom means looking to God, rather than human effort, as our ultimate source of everything we need for life. Our labor is not optional, but neither is it absolute. Our work, then, is always a participation in the grace of God's provision. In other words, despite what we are tempted to believe, jobs really are not our great providers; they are simply a means through which God cares for us.

Jesus demonstrates this principle before he teaches it in words. After a few particularly full days of ministry, Jesus withdraws with his inner circle to a city called Bethsaida. But word gets out and the crowds follow them. So Christ responds as he always has—he continues to teach about the kingdom of God and to heal those in need.

When the sun begins to set and his disciples realize the crowds aren't leaving, they grow concerned about how to feed them. They decide they better give Jesus some advice: "Send the crowd away, so that they may go into the surrounding villages and country-side, to lodge and get provisions; for we are here in a deserted place" (Luke 9:12). But Christ looks at the mass of humanity—at least five thousand strong—and has another idea. He knows of another source of provision, and so tells his disciples, "You give them something to eat."

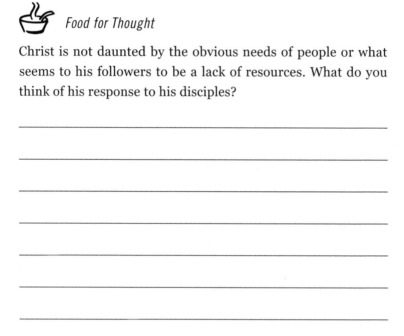 *Food for Thought*

Christ is not daunted by the obvious needs of people or what seems to his followers to be a lack of resources. What do you think of his response to his disciples?

_____

_____

_____

_____

_____

_____

_____

_____

Turning Ordinary into Extra

When his followers respond that they have only five loaves of bread and two fish, not nearly enough to feed themselves let alone the crowd, Jesus gives them a strange command. He has them use their professional skills—public administration (tax collectors) and food service (fishermen)—to organize the people into groups and get ready to serve them dinner. When they do, he takes the bread and fish, blesses them, and gives them to the disciples, who feed everyone there with twelve baskets left over!

Jesus makes use of ordinary food, and by God's power it becomes enough to feed several thousand. He incorporates, rather than replaces, the ordinary human means of providing food and the results are miraculous. Put another way, God in the person of Jesus takes responsibility for meeting the crowd's need for food and invites his followers to participate with him in the miracle. The result shows God's commitment to provide for his people. He doesn't have to tell them anything other than what to do—with him.

 Food for Thought

As humans, our work can do good or do harm. But when we respond as Jesus directs us, the result can be extraordinary. As Luke often reminds us throughout his Gospel, God can bring miraculous results out of our seemingly ordinary or insignificant offerings. In what ways has God provided for you, and how could you offer him your "loaves and fish"?

_____

_____

_____

_____

_____

_____

_____

Prayer

Pause to reflect in silence on God's many provisions in Christ. Then offer a prayer, either spontaneous or by using the following:

> *Dear God,*
>
> *You alone are able to supply our needs. Thank you for your promise of provision, fulfilled in the work of your people in the power of Jesus Christ.*
>
> *Amen.*

Lesson #2: A Lot Less Worry (Luke 12:22–33)

Why Worry?

After Jesus feeds the multitudes and shows them God's commitment to meeting their needs, he offers these words to live by.

> "I tell you, do not worry about your life, what you will eat, or about your body, what you will wear. . . . Can any of you by worrying add a single hour to your span of life? If then you are not able to do so small a thing as that, why do you worry about the rest?"
>
> (Luke 12:22, 25–26)

By pointing to God's provision even for the birds of the air, Jesus is giving what some might call a commonsense lesson. Worrying can't add an extra second or dollar to our lives, so why bother? Notice, though, that he doesn't say not to work—only not to worry about whether our work will provide enough to meet our needs.

In an economy of plenty, we would do well to take Christ's words to heart. Too many of us, however, are driven by worry to labor long hours in jobs we don't necessarily like, keeping us from enjoying our lives and neglecting the needs of those around us. Too often, our fretting seems to be about getting "enough" money to feel secure. But Christ makes it clear that no amount of money brings us genuine security.

 Food for Thought

Instead of worrying about earning more, as if we were our own providers, Christ teaches his followers to "strive [or seek] for his kingdom, and these things will be given to you as well" (Luke 12:31). Why do you think Jesus says that seeking the kingdom of God is an antidote to worry?

_____

_____

_____

_____

_____

_____

Blessed Assurance

If the ultimate goal in our lives and our work is God's kingdom, then we can live with the assurance that our goal will be met. God's promise of provision, made certain from the days of the Old Testament into Christ's time on earth and throughout history, is our anchor. We don't need to worry, if we are assured of the reality that God will indeed provide.

With that kind of confidence, we realize that our salaries are indeed enough because God is the one providing for our needs. As we recognize God's provision in our lives, we also become more aware of what others throughout the world might not have. After all, about a third of the world's population lives on less than a thousand dollars a year. And truth be told, it is difficult to reconcile the hard fact of poverty or starvation with God's promise of provision.

Surely, Jesus understood this tension as well. It's little wonder he also told his followers to "sell your possessions, and give alms" (Luke 12:33). Imagine what could happen if all of Christ's followers today used their work and wealth to alleviate or prevent poverty. In the process, we would become the means of God's provision for the poor.

 Food for Thought

As we consider the broader needs of people throughout the world, our "worries" are put into perspective and our hearts respond to Christ's leading. In what ways do you sense God might be calling you to become a source of provision for others?

Prayer

Pause to reflect in silence on the tension of God's assurance in a world with real poverty. Then offer a prayer, either spontaneous or by using the following:

Lord Jesus,

Thank you that you became poor for our sakes that we might be rich in good deeds. Help us to seek first your kingdom so others might know you as the Great Provider.

Amen.

Lesson #3: A Lot More Spending (Luke 16:1–13)

Building Cushions

The key to genuine security about the things we need is not to be anxious about what we earn or save, but to be wise stewards of God's provision. We are to spend ourselves on behalf of others, as Christ did, to be trustworthy servants of God because he is our provider.

Sometimes, though, that takes a little ingenuity, which seems to be at the heart of the parable of the dishonest manager. Here we have a manager who knows he is about to be fired for squandering the company's property. So he uses his last days on the job to make life a little easier for himself when he's unemployed. He doesn't try to embezzle enough to live on after he gets fired—he knows he could never get away with that. Instead, he calls in certain customers who owe the company and reduces their bills, hoping they'll return the favor down the road.

Christ uses the parable to reinforce that we cannot take anything with us when we depart this life. Obviously, we live in a world with market crashes, thefts, lawsuits, wars, and diseases—things we cannot control. So while building up great savings might seem wise, it offers no lasting security. Instead, Jesus instructs us to spend our wealth providing for others and depending on them to do the same when the need arises for us.

 Food for Thought

By providing for his master's debtors, the dishonest manager in the parable creates relationships, which the story implies is more effective for gaining security than the pursuit of wealth. How does this speak to you today, and what else can you learn from the parable?

_____

_____

_____

_____

_____

_____

_____

The Principle of Generosity

We first observed Jesus' emphasis on generosity when we explored the parable of the prodigal son. It comes up again strongly in the parable of the dishonest manager. Notice how he uses his master's money to create relationships. Apparently even buying people's favor with ill-gotten gain is better than having no relationships at all. When you have relationships and your life suddenly takes a turn you didn't expect, at least you'll have someone you can ask for help.

Even so, Jesus is not saying to depend on the fickle sentiments of those we've helped over the years. The story quickly turns from the debtors to the master in the story as the Lord endorses the master's maxim, "Whoever is faithful in a very little is faithful also in much" (Luke 16:10). God regards our generosity to other people as faithfulness to him. Even better, being generous creates in us a desire for a better relationship with God. Good relationships, both with God and with other people, produce good fruit, which strengthens our ability to build better relationships and create opportunities to be generous to others. If God entrusts us with a little, and we use it generously, he will entrust us with greater resources.

The parable ends with a clear distinction for managers and servants alike—we cannot serve two masters. "For a slave will either hate the one and love the other, or be devoted to the one and despise the other. You cannot serve God and wealth" (Luke 16:13). In other words, only when we decide to use our labor and our resources to serve God's purposes instead of making ourselves rich, will we be able to develop and truly be filled with the love of God.

 Food for Thought

The parable of the dishonest manager challenges our thinking about investing in others and inviting opportunities for generosity and hospitality. It is set in the workplace. What would it mean to be generous with the people you work with, for, and among?

Is generosity only about money, or does it also have to do with time, skill, compassion, and social inclusion? What could you do this week to act more generously?

_____

_____

_____

_____

_____

_____

_____

_____

Prayer

Pause to reflect in silence on the relationships God has provided for you on your journey. Then offer a prayer, either spontaneous or by using the following:

Gracious God,

Please help me to be faithful with all the resources you have given me as I share with others for your sake. Thank you for the debt that Jesus paid on the cross for my sake.

Amen.

Chapter 6

God's Kingdom and True Wealth

Lesson #1: The Myth of Wealth (Luke 12:13–21, 34)

Rich Deceits

With the promise of God's provision for his people, it might be easy to create a wish list for riches and wealth. It doesn't help that many people elevate wealth to the point that its pursuit and accumulation becomes an end in itself. And though Jesus has nothing against wealth, he is clearly suspicious of it. Just as work that reflects the life of Christ must exhibit a profound concern for others and an unwillingness to use power for self-gain, so also must wealth be an extension of our concern for our neighbors.

The problem is that having riches can be deceptive. It can quickly replace God, as Jesus says in Luke 12:34, "Where your treasure is, there your heart will be also." Wealth too often leads us to resist to any transformation in our lives, because it gives us the means to do things our own way for as long as we want.

But Luke repeatedly shows us how Christ wants people to recognize that they are defined, not by what they possess, but by their relationships with God and other people. And Jesus doesn't hold back on challenging the idolatry of wealth. "What does it profit them if they gain the whole world, but lose or forfeit themselves?" (Luke 9:25). He knows that the wealthy too often believe that their riches are sufficient and are therefore easily lured away from a personal relationship with God Almighty.

 Food for Thought

The Gospel of Luke challenges many of us about the ways we use our wealth. What does Christ's maxim "Where your treasure is, there your heart will be also" reveal to you? Where does your treasure say your heart must be? Does having money sometimes make it possible for you to avoid the hard work of maintaining good relationships with God and other people?

_____

_____

_____

_____

_____

_____

Rich Fools

A quick glance through the newspaper on any given day can show the foolish deeds of men and women who thought money was the answer to their problems. Financial greed in today's culture is not hard to spot. Sometimes it's criminal, such as convincing people to invest in fraudulent stocks. Sometimes it's much more subtle, such as thinking that a pay raise or a higher-paying job will solve our loneliness, self-doubt, or relationship problems.

But this is not new. The parable in Luke 12:13–21 shows a rich man who is not content with what he has. He wants more. Though his land produced abundantly, his barns can't hold everything. So he decides to tear them down and build bigger ones. He mistakenly believes that having more wealth will bring less worry about money, until of course something far greater comes—death. The wealth he counted on to satisfy him cannot control the reality of death, nor is his money his own any longer. It will be passed on to someone else, and what he prepared for himself—that is, a life without God—now means true death.

The rich fool thought his possessions would make him secure, but Jesus shows how futile wealth is if we do not use it to love God and serve other people. Yet the man never even considered using his crops to provide for those in need. "So it is with those who store up treasures for themselves but are not rich toward God" (Luke 12:21). Their money does no one good, not even themselves.

 Food for Thought

Friendship with God is seen here in economic terms. God's friends who are rich provide for God's friends who are poor. The rich fool's problem was that he hoarded things for himself—not producing jobs or prosperity for others—and loved his money more than God or his people. How can you use money and other things you have to bring prosperity to others? Is giving money part of the answer? How much? Is giving money the entire answer?

_____

_____

_____

_____

_____

Prayer

Pause to reflect in silence on the treasures God has placed in your heart. Then offer a prayer, either spontaneous or by using the following:

Merciful God,

It is too easy to be greedy for more. Instead help me to use what I have to draw close to Christ and to be satisfied that he is enough.

Amen.

Lesson #2: The Purpose of Wealth (Luke 18:18–30)

Giving and Investing for People in Need

Riches can make our lives so comfortable that they distract us from what is most important—following Christ. What we need to remember is that every penny with which we have been entrusted has a purpose. If individuals who love God are wealthy, we may often find them holding their wealth lightly and giving liberally to those in need. Other times we see them investing their money to develop goods or services that benefit other people, or to create good jobs, or to bring justice to vulnerable people.

The point of the economic blessings we receive is not to amass our own empires but to give to others as we work toward God's kingdom. So when we come to the story of the rich ruler in Luke 18, we can appreciate the tension in his exchange with Jesus. In fact, his story points to the possibility of redemption from the grip of wealth. Why? Because he has not let his riches obliterate his desire for God.

He asks what he must do to inherit eternal life, and Christ responds with a summary of the Ten Commandments. "I have kept all these since my youth," he replies (Luke 18:21). Jesus seems to accept him at his word, yet notices something else at work in the ruler—wealth's subtle but corrupting influence.

 Food for Thought

For those whose hearts desire God's will, economic wealth can be a tool for good. What are ways you have used your money for good? For evil? What gives money such power for good or for evil?

_____

_____

_____

_____

_____

_____

Unmatched Generosity

When Jesus challenges the rich ruler to "sell all that you own and distribute the money to the poor, and you will have treasure in heaven" (Luke 18:22), he is offering him a way to end wealth's destructive influence. He is inviting the ruler to something far more fulfilling—intimacy with him. Those with a deep desire for God will respond wholeheartedly to an invitation to daily personal intimacy with their Maker. But with the rich ruler, Jesus perceives that it's too late, because his love of wealth has exceeded his love for God.

We know this because Luke then tells us the ruler "became sad; for he was very rich" (Luke 18:23). Christ responds with even more difficult words: "How hard it is for those who have wealth to enter the kingdom of God! Indeed, it is easier for a camel to go through the eye of a needle than for someone who is rich to enter the kingdom of God" (Luke 18:25).

Unlike the ruler, a poor widow later in Luke (21:1–4) is able to give away all she has because of her for love for God. And the poor often show amazing generosity. In contrast, though, the people standing near the ruler recognize wealth's seductive power and wonder if anyone can resist it. Thankfully, Jesus has an answer for them as well. "What is impossible for mortals is possible for God" (Luke 18:27).

 Food for Thought

God himself is the source of strength for those who desire to love him more than wealth. And as we do, we'll find our desire will grow and enable us to live with radical generosity. What might seem impossible to you right now that is possible for God?

_____

_____

_____

_____

_____

_____

_____

Prayer

Pause to reflect in silence on what it would mean to give away your possessions. Then offer a prayer, either spontaneous or by using the following:

Dear God,

Help me to love you more than wealth or things. Thank you that you have provided treasure for me by intimacy with you through Jesus.

Amen.

Lesson #3: The Real Legacy of Wealth (Luke 12:33; 16:19–31)

Rich Priorities

Don Flow owns a series of car dealerships in the American southeast. While comparing profit margins on various sales transactions, he discovered that low-income customers were paying higher prices on average than higher-income customers. He realized that low-income customers had less experience with negotiation and were more intimidated by salespeople. So he decided to remove negotiation from the sales process. He calculated the maximum discount he was willing to give on every car and then posted that price on the car. Now everyone pays the same price for the same car.

This practice means his car dealerships have a lower profit margin because they give the lowest price even to people who are poor negotiators. But it is fairer, especially to the poorest customers, so Don decided it was the right thing to do. It also creates great relationships with customers. So Don has plenty of repeat business.

According to Jesus, a practice like this might also create a closer relationship with God. "Make purses for yourselves that do not wear out, an unfailing treasure in heaven, where no thief comes near and no moth destroys" (Luke 12:33). Don Flow made his relationship with wealth far less important than the relationships that did not "wear out"—such as fair relationships with customers. Christ's priorities had become his, and becoming more like Christ brings us closer to God.

 Food for Thought

It's hard to make changes that put our money or possessions at risk, even when they're the right thing to do. We can always come up with an argument about why the old way was okay. But if we change the question from "Is what I'm doing okay?" to "How can I use the things I have to become more like Christ?" then we open up a new world of possibilities. What could you do differently in your work that would make things fairer for people at the bottom? How much risk would it cost you? Would it be worth it? Would it truly bring you closer to God? If you can't do this today, how could you do so in the future?

Lasting Concerns

As we know, not all who are rich hoard their wealth or spend it only on themselves. Many give generously of their time and resources to others, and they give special attention to helping people in poverty. Such concern for others reflects God's persistent concern for the poor and powerless, which we see throughout Luke's Gospel.

Jesus brings this idea to a powerful point in the parable of Lazarus and the rich man in Luke 16:19–31. Here the rich man lives in luxury and indulges every desire, doing nothing to relieve Lazarus, who is dying of hunger and disease. When both die, we're reminded that wealth has no great power after all. The angels carry Lazarus to heaven, apparently for no reason other than his poverty, or perhaps because his love for God had never been displaced by wealth. The rich man goes to Hades, apparently because his greed kept him from loving God or others.

The parable certainly implies that the rich man's duty was to care for the needs of those who had nothing. If he had shown such concern, he might have made things right with God and avoided his miserable end. But he, like the rest of his family who remain alive, was so consumed with his own riches that he would not change his ways "even if someone rises from the dead" (Luke 16:31) to warn him. Even Jesus himself—the one who rises from the dead—can be ignored by those who care nothing for God or people.

 Food for Thought

God's character is formed in those who love him before riches, and consequently they become generous toward others. Their duty to care for the poor and powerless becomes a joy and a privilege because it's grounded in God's love. What practical steps can you take to become more loving toward poor and powerless people?

_____

_____

_____

_____

_____

_____

_____

_____

Prayer

Pause to reflect in silence on Christ's words in Luke 6:20,

"Blessed are you who are poor,
    for yours is the kingdom of God."

Then offer a prayer, either spontaneous or by using the following:

Lord Jesus,

Thank you for the many gifts and opportunities you give me to serve others with your joy and compassion. Please help me to be your hands in caring for poor people and your voice for those who are powerless.

Amen.

Chapter 7

God's Kingdom and Countercultural Leadership

Lesson #1: Humble Positions (Luke 9:46–48; 22:24–30)

A Posture of Good

As Luke records Christ's life and ministry, he focuses on consistent themes of justice and compassion, healing and grace. In other words, all of Christ's life is spent caring for others, a cornerstone of God's kingdom.

So when we begin to look at Christ as a leader, we can't help but see a posture of humility. Whenever Jesus exercises leadership or power, he does so for God's purposes rather than his own self-interest. Likewise, as Christians are called to lead and to exercise power, we must heed Christ's posture and teachings.

Humble service to others, then, is one of the greatest marks of the Christian life and a joyful privilege. But when his disciples began arguing over who would be the greatest in God's kingdom, Jesus was blunt about their mixed-up perceptions. The greatest, he said, is the one who welcomes not a CEO or world leader but a child in his name. "For the least among all of you is the greatest" (Luke 9:48). The model here is not the child but the person who welcomes a child, because serving those whom others might consider insignificant is what makes a leader great.

Food for Thought

Greatness in God's kingdom looks very different from how our culture might define it. Leadership in God's kingdom looks different too. What contrasts do you see between the perspectives of contemporary culture and God's kingdom?

_____

_____

_____

_____

_____

_____

_____

_____

Pointing to Others (Luke 22:24–30)

Another dispute arose among Christ's followers about who was going to be regarded as the greatest. How often our egos get in the way of our work! Too frequently we want to put ourselves before others or gain recognition for this project or that account, rather than making someone else look good. Our first inclination is often to take credit for everything. But Christ confronts this with profoundly radical words:

> "The kings of the Gentiles lord it over them; and those in authority over them are called benefactors. But not so with you; rather the greatest among you must become like the youngest, and the leader like one who serves. For who is greater, the one who is at the table or the one who serves? Is it not the one at the table? But I am among you as one who serves." (Luke 22:25–27)

Here, Jesus turns the perceived notion of leadership on its head and models leading by serving. Such humility seeks opportunities to bring healing, dignity, and justice to others, no matter what it might cost him as a leader. In other words, effective leadership is service. It's elevating others at your own expense.

 Food for Thought

When we try to take credit for good deeds or work, others are less likely to follow us. But when we point out the accomplishments of others, our posture of humility and grace attracts respect and loyalty. How does our Lord's posture of service inspire you in your career?

_____

_____

_____

_____

_____

Prayer

Pause to reflect in silence on Christ's words, "I am among you as one who serves." Then offer a prayer, either spontaneous or by using the following:

Lord,

Thank you for becoming weak for our sakes, and for giving up your power on the cross so that we might know the great joy of serving others. Empower me through your Spirit to point others to you.

Amen.

Lesson #2: Unexpected Moments (Luke 14:7–24)

Kingdom Faux Pas

Imagine being invited to a company party where the entire staff is present, including all the vice presidents and the CEO. You're still in the entry-level position for which you were hired but think this might be a good chance to get ahead, to approach some key people who can help put in a good word for that promotion. So you begin to work the room to talk about how your qualifications aren't being fully utilized, but soon people grow chilly toward you.

This is what's happening in the parable of the banquet, and Jesus is not impressed. In fact, he considers this type of self-promotion a waste of time, a counterproductive action. Why? Because, as he puts it, "all who exalt themselves will be humbled" (Luke 14:11).

The better approach is to be patient, offering others your place at the table or in the buffet line. It is a chance to affirm others and to put them ahead of your own interests. Making the people around you look good is more likely to help you achieve your goals than trying to make yourself look good. As Jesus said, "Those who humble themselves will be exalted."

 Food for Thought

Leadership at work, as Christ defines it, is serving others and putting them ahead of our own interests in each situation in which we find ourselves. It requires honest humility. How might your own ego or pride be keeping you from serving others for Christ's sake?

_____

_____

_____

_____

Who's Coming?

The next part of this passage in Luke 14 takes another unusual twist. Not only does Christ provide instruction about humbling ourselves so that others might be honored, but he also reminds us that just as with wealth and riches, it is a generous spirit toward others that counters any sense of selfishness in our work.

In some ways, generosity can be seen as God's secret weapon. If by God's power we begin to care more for others, serving them and giving to those in need, then we also begin to experience the kingdom as Christ described it. Generosity can mean giving to others or serving others with no expectation of return.

In this parable of the wedding banquet, Jesus challenges his listeners to create a guest list no one would dream of, and tells them not to invite their friends or family or rich neighbors. Instead, we should invite "the poor, the crippled, the lame, and the blind" (Luke 14:13). When we do, he says, everyone—including us—will be blessed because they cannot repay us. A generous leader, then, is one who puts others first and who expects nothing in return when giving.

 ### Food for Thought

True generosity and service—the kind that does not expect to be paid back in this life—is countercultural and breaks the hold that greed or power can have on us. It is formed in our lives because we have a reward of another kind, the reward of the resurrection. How does the hope of eternal life with God change how you care for others now, especially those individuals on the margins?

_____

_____

_____

_____

_____

_____

_____

_____

Prayer

Pause to reflect in silence on all God has done for you. Then offer a prayer, either spontaneous or by using the following:

Gracious God,

You have generously given us eternal life through Christ's sacrifice on the cross and his resurrection. Help me to give back to you by freely serving the people you have put in my life today.

Amen.

Lesson #3: True Power (Luke 19:1–10; 20:20–26)

God's Rule

Throughout his Gospel, Luke has identified Jesus as the one who is bringing God's rule to earth. At first people welcome him as God's king. When he rides into town, people line the streets singing, "Blessed is the king who comes in the name of the Lord!" (Luke 19:38). But the type of rule and power he claims as Messiah is not necessarily what the people expect. In only a few days the crowd will turn on him and shout, "Crucify, crucify him!" (Luke 23:21).

Christ the king, however, does not change. Instead, he shows true power by transforming people in the power structures around him. That's what happens when Jesus encounters a tax collector named Zacchaeus, who's sitting in a tree to get a better view of the Lord as he passes. Tax collectors weren't exactly popular in the Roman provinces, because they frequently overcharged people on their taxes. And to subjugated people such as the Jews, tax collectors were a daily reminder of Roman tyranny. So it's no small thing that Jesus stops on the road, looks up at Zacchaeus, and tells him, "I must stay at your house today" (Luke 19:5).

Zacchaeus obliges and his life is profoundly changed. No longer will he use his power as a tax collector to intimidate others or deceive them about their taxes. Instead, as a civil servant and worker now of God's kingdom, he publically announces Christ's power over him and promises, "Look, half of my possessions, Lord, I will give to the poor; and if I have defrauded anyone of anything, I will pay back four times as much" (Luke 19:8). In response, Jesus says, "Today salvation has come to this house" (Luke 19:9).

 Food for Thought

Zacchaeus is changed because Christ invites him into personal relationship with him. Because he is now a servant of God's king, he can no longer engage in business practices contrary to God's ways. What does the story of Zacchaeus teach you about Christ's power or "rule" in your life and profession?

_____

_____

_____

_____

God's Due

After Jesus is welcomed as king in Jerusalem, the teachers of the law and chief priests try to "trap him by what he said, so as to hand him over to the jurisdiction and authority of the governor" (Luke 20:20). They ask whether it's lawful to pay taxes to Caesar, and Christ responds by looking at a coin and telling them to "give to the emperor the things that are the emperor's, and to God the things that are God's" (Luke 20:25).

Some might think Jesus is separating the material world from the spiritual in his answer, but he is not. In fact, he's not suggesting that Caesar's world is different from God's. This would not be consistent with everything Christ has been saying throughout Luke. After all, what is God's? Everything! So whatever may belong to Caesar also belongs to God. Taxes, government, production, leadership positions, banquets, and every other kind of work are exactly the areas into which God's kingdom comes. Christians in all positions and vocations are called to engage the world, not drop out of it. All that a follower of Christ does—from serving and giving to leading and affirming—must point to the God who makes all things possible. When we do, Christ's rule in each aspect of our lives spills over into every conversation and becomes an opportunity to give God his due.

 *Food for Thought*

Jesus comes into the world as king, and that historic reality is God's claim that the entire world is his. How does your faith in Christ's lordship change how you do your work?

_____

_____

_____

_____

_____

_____

_____

_____

Prayer

Pause in silence to reflect on the true power of Christ as king and his countercultural leadership. Then offer a prayer, either spontaneous or by using the following:

God of the Universe,

You rule over every part of the earth, yet Christ gave up power on the cross for my sake. Help me to honor you in all I do and say.

Amen.

Chapter 8

God's Kingdom and Life's Passion

Lesson #1: Losing Passion (Luke 23:34, 44–49)

Ultimate Sacrifice

Ask a group of people how they would define the word *passion* and you'll likely get a variety of answers. A quick look at the history of the word, however, shows that it evolved from the Passion of Christ, where it meant to suffer with intensity.

Throughout Luke's Gospel, we have watched Jesus extend grace and healing to those in need, while also confronting religious leaders with his truth and wisdom. In short, he is establishing his work as king and building his kingdom—his new culture and way of exercising power—in the world around us. With each step and each interaction, though, Jesus is also making enemies. He disrupts the status quo, and those in power at present do not take it lightly. They will do anything to stop him.

Christ is therefore turned over to the authorities who are just "doing their job." He is tried, convicted, beaten, and sent to execution on a cross—an excruciating form of capital punishment. And in his final dark moments of suffering on that cross, we see a king who seems to be losing his kingdom and power.

 *Food for Thought*

Jesus died a slow death between two criminals in front of a large crowd outside of town. Yet on the cross, Luke tells us that Christ said, "Father, forgive them; for they do not know what they are doing" (Luke 23:34). What do you think his followers must have thought as they watched their king on the cross and heard his prayer? Are these the words of a king? To put it another way, what kind of kingdom has a ruler who would say this while being killed by his own subjects?

_____

_____

_____

_____

_____

_____

_____

The Point

The climax of Christ's work during his time on earth is finished when he breathes his last. In a gasp, he exclaims his trust in God: "Father, into your hands I commend my spirit" (Luke 23:46). He is willing to sacrifice his life on the cross and able to trust God to what seemed like the end.

Yet through his death and the Father's mighty deed of resurrection, Jesus passes fully into the position of eternal king foretold at his birth. "The Lord God will give to him the throne of his ancestor David. He will reign over the house of Jacob forever, and of his kingdom there will be no end" (Luke 1:32–33). Truly, this is God's beloved Son, faithful unto death as he works on behalf of all of us who have fallen into the poverty of sin and death, in need of a redemption we can't provide ourselves.

In this light, we see that Christ's care for the poor and the powerless is both an end in itself and a sign of his love for everyone who will follow him. We are all poor and powerless in the face of our own sin and the world's brokenness. Yet in his resurrection we find ourselves transformed in every aspect of life and caught up in God's extravagant love where true passion is redeemed.

 Food for Thought

Christ the King gave up his power on the cross by taking on our sins. How can his extravagant love and passion for you lead you today?

_____

_____

_____

_____

_____

_____

_____

_____

Prayer

Pause in silence to reflect on Christ's ultimate sacrifice for you and for those around you. Then offer a prayer, either spontaneous or by using the following:

> *O Lord,*
>
> *In your darkness on the cross you brought me into the light of life. May my life reflect your great sacrifice and love.*
>
> *Amen.*

Lesson #2: Walking with Jesus (Luke 24:13–35)

Good News

After Christ rose from the dead, he spent forty days walking the earth, very much alive, and extending the same grace and generosity he had before his death. He talked with women and ate with his close friends and followers, appearing to over five hundred people, according to the Apostle Paul (1 Cor. 15:6).

He also walked on busy roads with them. In fact, the story we come to now in Luke 24:13–35 of the Emmaus road is a fitting example of Christ's ongoing generosity. At first glance, Cleopas and his friend seem to take Christ's death too lightly when they begin a conversation with the man beside them. "Are you the only stranger in Jerusalem who does not know the things that have taken place there in these days?" (Luke 24:18). It's not hard to imagine Cleopas adding, "What rock have you been living under?"

Jesus, though, takes it in stride and listens as they talk. When they finish, he turns the tables and invites them to listen to what was likely one of the greatest history lessons in all of Scripture. Eventually, the light begins to dawn on them that perhaps the women's story of their Messiah's miraculous resurrection might not be as crazy as they thought!

 Food for Thought

Little is known of Cleopas and his companion, yet Christ appears intentionally to these two seemingly insignificant characters in the story of his resurrection. What does that communicate about his mission and what do you think it would have been like listening to his lesson?

_____

_____

_____

_____

_____

_____

_____

_____

Returning the Favor

Before and after his death, Christ invited others into fellowship with him and his followers. He modeled hospitality on every level, an attribute that has marked the Christian life and church throughout history.

Yet it is interesting to note that the two disciples on the Emmaus road seem at first not to understand just who is talking with them. "Oh, how foolish you are, and how slow of heart to believe all that the prophets have declared!" Jesus says to them (Luke 24:25). And they could be forgiven, considering how unprecedented his resurrection is. Still, they do one thing right—they offer hospitality back to Jesus.

They say to him, "Stay with us, because it is almost evening and the day is now nearly over" (Luke 24:29). As a result, Jesus blesses this small act of generosity with the revelation of his presence. In the breaking of the bread they at last recognize him (Luke 24:30–31). Likewise, when we offer hospitality to others, God uses it not only as a means of serving those in need of refreshment but also as an invitation for us to experience Christ's presence ourselves.

 Food for Thought

Part of participating in the life, passion, and resurrection of Jesus is to extend to others the same grace and kindness we have received from him. In what ways—simple or sacrificial—can you offer hospitality to those with whom you interact daily?

_____

_____

_____

_____

_____

_____

_____

Prayer

Pause in silence to reflect on the simple walk the resurrected Lord took with two friends. Then offer a prayer, either spontaneous or by using the following:

Dear God,

Thank you that you pursue us in the seemingly ordinary moments of our lives and give us opportunities to reflect back to others your amazing gift of refreshment in our acts of hospitality.

Amen.

Lesson #3: Jesus' Kingdom Continues (Luke 10:27–28; 24:44–48)

Living the Story

Luke's Gospel is the story of how God's kingdom emerged on earth in the person of God's king, Jesus Christ. We have watched him at work as an unconventional ruler, healing the sick, feeding the hungry, challenging the culture, and giving his life for others, both in death and in resurrection. His authority as king is defined by humility, service, and grace. And as the true king of the world, Christ is both the ruler to whom we owe our allegiance and the model for how we are to exercise whatever authority we are given in this life.

So how can today's followers of Christ continue living his story? Let's return to his words in Luke 10:27–28 when he gives us one great commandment in two parts: "You shall love the Lord your God with all your heart, and with all your soul, and with all your strength, and with all your mind; and your neighbor as yourself. . . . Do this, and you will live." It is not a new commandment but a summary of the Law of Moses. What is new is that the kingdom based on this law has been inaugurated through God's incarnation in the person of Jesus!

God's intent from the beginning was for us to live in his kingdom. But from the time of Adam and Eve's sin onwards, people have lived instead in the kingdom of darkness and evil. Jesus comes to reclaim the earth as God's kingdom and to create a community of God's people who live under his rule, even while the kingdom of darkness retains much of its sway.

 Food for Thought

Our citizenship in Christ's kingdom means that we live all of our lives—including work—in pursuit of the purposes of his kingdom and according to his ways. What specific guidance has Luke's Gospel provided for you as God's citizen in your work?

_____

_____

_____

_____

_____

_____

_____

_____

Life Indeed

In the last chapter of Luke, the resurrected Lord says to his followers what he has been telling them all along—everything written about him in the Law of Moses, the prophets, and the psalms is fulfilled. Then he charges them with their new identity as witnesses of how Christ the King has fulfilled his role. He blesses them and sends them out. They, in turn, can't help but praise God (Luke 24:44–53).

Likewise, Jesus teaches us the purposes and ways of his kingdom. He calls us to work at tasks such as healing, justice, leadership, and productivity, as well as investments, government, generosity, and hospitality. And he sends God's Spirit to give us everything we need to fulfill our specific callings, promising always to provide for us. As he does, he commands us to provide for others, suggesting his provision for us will often come in the form of other people working on our behalf.

Yet he also warns us of the trap of believing that our own wealth makes us self-sufficient, and he shows that instead we must use wealth to further relationships with God and others. When conflicts arise in our relationships, the Prince of Peace teaches us how to resolve them so they lead to justice and reconciliation. Above all, he teaches that citizenship in God's kingdom means working as a servant of God and of people. His self-sacrifice on the cross serves as the ultimate model of servant leadership. His resurrection to the throne of God's kingdom confirms and establishes that the active love of our neighbor is the way of eternal life!

 *Food for Thought*

The commandment to love God and love our neighbors defines the abundant and eternal life we have received through Christ our king. What does it mean for you to love God with all your heart, soul, strength, and mind as you love your neighbor as yourself?

_____

_____

_____

_____

_____

_____

_____

_____

Prayer

Pause in silence to reflect on the extravagant love of Christ and the life he has called you to. Then offer a prayer, either spontaneous or by using the following:

O God,

We praise you for making us witnesses to the work of the Messiah, for forgiving our sins and empowering us to show others your love. Thank you for calling us to be citizens of your eternal kingdom.

Amen.

Wisdom for Using This Study in the Workplace

Community within the workplace is a good thing and a Christian community within the workplace is even better. Sensitivity is needed, however, when we get together in the workplace (even a Christian workplace) to enjoy fellowship time together, learn what the Bible has to say about our work, and encourage one another in Jesus' name. When you meet at your place of employment, here are some guidelines to keep in mind:

- *Be sensitive to your surroundings.* Know your company policy about having such a group on company property. Make sure not to give the impression that this is a secret or exclusive group.

- *Be sensitive to time constraints.* Don't go over your allotted time. Don't be late to work! Make sure you are a good witness to the others (especially non-Christians) in your workplace by being fully committed to your work during working hours and doing all your work with excellence.

- *Be sensitive to the shy or silent members of your group.* Encourage everyone in the group and give them a chance to talk.

- *Be sensitive to the others by being prepared.* Read the Bible study material and Scripture passages and think about your answers to the questions ahead of time.

These Bible studies are based on the *Theology of Work Bible Commentary*. Besides reading the commentary, please visit the Theology of Work website (www.theologyofwork.org) for videos, interviews, and other material on the Bible and your work.

Leader's Guide

Living Word. It is always exciting to start a new group and study. The possibilities of growth and relationship are limitless when we engage with one another and with God's word. Always remember that God's word is "living and active, sharper than any two-edged sword" (Heb. 4:12). When you study his word, it should change you.

A Way Has Been Made. Please know that you and each person joining your study have been prayed for by people you will probably never meet but who share your faith. And remember that it is "the Lord who goes before you. He will be with you; he will not fail you or forsake you. Do not fear or be dismayed" (Deut. 31:8). As a leader, you need to know that truth. Remind yourself of it throughout this study.

Pray. It is always a good idea to pray for your study and those involved weeks before you even begin. It is recommended that you pray for yourself as leader, your group members, and the time you are about to spend together. It's no small thing you are about to start and the more you prepare in the Spirit, the better. Apart from Jesus, we can do nothing. Remain in him and you will "bear much fruit" (John 15:5). It's also a good idea to have trusted friends pray and intercede for you and your group as you work through the study.

Spiritual Battle. Like it or not, the Bible teaches that we are in the middle of a spiritual battle. The enemy would like nothing more than for this study to be ineffective. It would be part of his scheme to have group members not show up or engage in any discussion. His victory would be that your group passes time together going through the motions of just another Bible study. You, as a leader, are a threat to the enemy as it is your desire to lead people down the path of righteousness (as taught in Proverbs). Read Ephesians 6:10–20 and put your armor on.

Scripture. Prepare before your study by reading the selected Scripture verses ahead of time.

Chapters. Each chapter contains three lessons. As you work through the lessons, keep in mind the particular chapter theme in connection with the lessons. These lessons are designed so that you can go through them in thirty minutes each.

Lessons. Each lesson has teaching points with their own discussion questions. This format should keep the participants engaged with the text and one another.

Food for Thought. The questions at the end of the teaching points are there to create discussion and deepen the connection between each person and the content being addressed. You know the people in your group and should feel free to come up with your own questions or adapt the ones provided to best meet the needs of your group. Again, this would require some preparation beforehand.

Opening and Closing Prayers. Sometimes prayer prompts are given before and usually after each lesson. These are just suggestions. You know your group and the needs present, so please feel free to pray accordingly.

Bible Commentary. The Theology of Work series contains a variety of books to help you apply the Scriptures and Christian faith to your work. This Bible study is based on the *Theology of Work Bible Commentary*, which examines what the Bible says about work. This commentary is intended to assist those with theological training or interest to conduct in-depth research into passages or books of Scripture.

Video Clips. The Theology of Work website (www.theologyofwork.com) provides good video footage of people from the marketplace highlighting teaching on work from every book of the Bible. It would be great to incorporate some of these videos into your teaching time.

Enjoy Your Study! Remember that God's word does not return void—ever. It produces fruit and succeeds in whatever way God has intended it to succeed.

> "So shall my word be that goes out from my mouth;
>   it shall not return to me empty,
>   but it shall accomplish that which I purpose,
>   and shall succeed in the thing for which I sent it." (Isa. 55:11)

Explore what the Bible has to say about work, book by book.

THE BIBLE AND YOUR WORK
Study Series

THEOLOGY OF WORK   PROJECT